SEX EDUCATION FOR 8-12 YEAR OLDS
KIDS BOOK FOR GOOD PARENTS

By Ana Leblanc

The trademarks that are used are without any consent, and the publication of the trademark is without permission or backing by the trademark owner. All trademarks and brands within this book are for clarifying purposes only and are the owned by the owners themselves, not affiliated with this document.

PREFACE

Parents ought to be the first source of sex education for their children. Don't think that because children can learn about human sexuality in school, your responsibility to teach them about sex has been removed. Especially now that there is confusion as to how to teach human sexuality in school, the parents must be ready to assume the role to educate their children in everything they need to know to understand their sexuality. This book serves as a guide for parents and guardians to educate their children on the issue of sex so they can understand the myths and facts about this important topic.

Table of Contents

CHAPTER 1 SEX EDUCATION CA BE EASY

Sex education has never been an issue with my children. The most important thing you need to know is to look for the everyday opportunities that present themselves and act upon them.

I can remember once being in a car with one of my sons. He was only 8 years old at the time, but was sitting beside a lady friend of mine who was very large breasted. My son said to me, "hey mum, look at this", and opened his mouth like he was going to suck on the lady's breast (as he had seen me breast feed three babies by then). I was mortified and said to David, "that's not the right thing to do, David". I didn't say anything else at the time as it wasn't appropriate. Luckily my friend was very understanding about the incident.

Later on when we were at home I said to him, "so you noticed that my friend has large breasts?" I know that he was only 8 years old but he had noticed something and didn't need to be ignored. Admittedly he went about things the wrong way but he was only eight years old. So I took the opportunity to say to him, "David as you grow older you are going to notice that many of your girlfriends will start to grow breasts. It's just a normal part of growing up. And it is important for you to make sure that when talk to girls you look at their faces and not at their breasts". We had a great conversation and I didn't make a big deal of it. But I did answer all of his ⬚uestions.

When my children were young I started their sex education by buying books for them. I found a great series of books for various age groups. When my kids were six I used the 6 to 8 year old book. I would read a chapter a night to them. It was a story book called "Where Do Babies Come From?" My kids would sit and listen to it as it was simply the routine they were in to at the time. As they got older we changed our tactics slightly.

Now, the books are in the book shelf for all to read whenever they so desire. I have made it a very natural thing for the kids to talk about sexual things and they feel comfortable asking questions. It is far better for you to answer your child's questions than to let them hear things from someone else, because that someone else will be their peers and peers don't always have the facts right. If you promote communication with your child they will come to you when they have questions.

Now my eldest son is fourteen and we have a great relationship. He can talk to me about absolutely anything and everything as I have paved the way for this to happen. If you want to have a great relationship with your child you must work hard to pave the way also which means making the most of every opportunity to communicate with your child about everything including sex. If you don't make it a taboo subject they will feel free to discuss things openly with you.

How to Educate Your Child About Sex

Many parents think that talking about sex in front of their kids may harm their brain and take them in the wrong way. But this is totally a misconception. Even avoidance of sex education can make more harm to the kids. You may adopt the following methods to educate your child about sex.

1. Try to teach sex to your child in a matter of fact manner, in the same manner as you, would talk about any matter with them.

2. Do not lecture. Be persuasive and sympathetic and make sure the child's interest remains sustained and element of curiosity stays on.

3. If a child poses any question, during the course of sex education, that must be replied to allay his doubts and/or misconceptions.

4. Your discussion should not be around disclosure of biological factors alone. It should also include values, emotions, decision making also, since the young ones value such qualities.

5. Puberty begins from the tenth year, when physical changes like pubic hair, erection of clitoris, enlargement of breast and prominence of nipples, menstruation etc start taking places. So, it is always better to educate the child about sex before the said changes surface.

6. Electronic media, porno magazines and literature, x-rated films have already enhanced children's knowledge about homosexuality,

heterosexuality, prostitution, masturbation, self-abuse or child-abuse, etc. So, such aspect must also be part of a parent's sex education program.

7. Tell your child what is erection of penis and of clitoris and also what is masturbation, especially to girls. Also explain how and when venereal diseases, AIDS, HIV problems set in. Respond to child's enquiries in a receptive, sympathetic and friendly way, so that they don't feel that they have been landed in an awkward position. Let them stay normal.

8. Include and encourage your child to put any question, concerning the subject, to you and, when asked, be simple explicit.

Advantage of teaching your chid sex education

Sex education is a very important aspect of growing up. There is a pressure,on children and teenagers to know. Life naturally mounts pressure on them to learn. They are naturally inquisitive. They want to learn anything within their environment. Since these categories of people are curious and want to learn anything, it is therefore paramount to teach them. Whether they are thought at home or not they will learn. So it is very important to teach them at home instead of them to learn from their peer group.

The right age to start teaching your children sex education is between eight and twelve years. In this age or period, there will be physical or Biological changes in them which will naturally trigger out the consciousness to find out the causes, reasons, and needs for the Biological changes.

It is, therefore, a good idea to teach them at home so that they will not learn from their friends. Even if they will learn from their friends, they should first of all learn it at home so that they will know when they are being mislead.

Sex education is more important to girls than their male folks. Every girl should be able to know many if not all of the disadvantages of sex to a growing up girl, at the age of twelve. The biological changes or physical changes that take place in the girl child at this particular period are stimulants to sex. They will be attracted to boys or men.

Boys or men, who are interested to see everything in skirt, except the God fearing ones will want to use every trick possible to take girls to bed. Girls are thrilled by words of admiration from boy and men. Girls are delighted to hear I love you from the opposite sex. So, if sex education is not given to them by their parents, they will be victims of sexual abuse.

What they need to know

That all living things reproduce the basic facts about sex, conception, pregnancy, and the birth process.

That there are many different types of family situations and that no single type is better than the rest.

They can live outside of stereotyped gender roles – for example, that women can be good leaders and men can be good at taking care of children.

That sexual identity includes sexual orientation.

That we must all take an active role in protecting our health.

The basic facts about disease prevention.

That a friend is someone we enjoy being with, someone who shares, listens, encourages, and helps us think through our problems.

How to develop, maintain, and end friendships

How to recognize and protect themselves from potential sexual abuse – for example, children need to know that sexual predators may seem kind, giving, and loving. They may be friends or family members.

Puberty Education

Puberty is the most crucial stage of our lives and everyone goes through it at some point in life. All the major changes, physical, emotional and psychological occur during this stage. A human body starts developing as one moves from childhood to adolescence. It has been scientifically proved that girls mature earlier as compared to boys. Girls get their first period around 12 years of age, i.e., two to two and half years after they begin puberty. But, this is a general observation, it differs from one girl to another. Some girls might get their first period as early as

9 years of age and as late as age 16. Naturally, the changes in girls are different from boys and so the timing of puberty varies a great deal in both of them. Puberty in girls starts between the ages 8 and 13 whereas in boys it is between 10 and 15 years. The wide age range can answer your question, why some girls and boys of your child's age still look like kids and some look more like adults.

The beginning of puberty at a very early stage is called precocious puberty. All individuals cannot take these changes easily as others and might be frightened and confused about it. Some schools talk to their students about these topics, but it comes very late. It is the primary responsibility of the parents to talk to their children during their early childhood, approximately at the age of 8 years. The next segment is divided into two parts because the ways to talk to girls and boys about puberty are different.

Talking to Your Daughter About Puberty

Earlier, the situation was somewhat like this: when a girl gets her first period, only then she knows about it. The mother or any other elderly female never bothered to explain what it exactly was or why it happens? The girl was not supposed to ask questions about it and even if she asked, very casual and ridiculous answers like "it happens" or "every girl goes through it" were given to her and nothing more than that. What should she makes out of such statements? The girl used to feel only confused and helpless. But, nowadays, the situation has changed. Children are exposed to so many things that they are aware of these things before the right time and the information is also not from the reliable sources. Thanks to the present media and television. These mediums have become so much independent that they take up any issue and present it as they want. In such, a scenario, talking about the issues of puberty remains an important point and you as a parent, should be very careful and start talking, as early as possible, to your daughter about puberty. Here are afew tips to help you initiate the talk on this sensitive yet most important subject with your daughter.

Let her know about menstruation even before she gets her first period otherwise she will be frightened at the sight and location of the blood. You can start talking to her right from the age of 8 years.

Convince her that it is absolutely natural and normal, and everyone has to go through it sometime in life, only the timing differs from person to person. It is very important to convince her on this part because if your girl is alone in her group who still did not get her first period or if she is the first one to get it, she might feel embarrassed and as an odd man out.

Tell her the reason behind the small lumps that she experiences around her nipples and about the swelling of the breasts. Let her know that her body is growing according to her age and the above-mentioned parts are the major organs that reflect the changes in the growth prominently.

The growth of hair in the armpits and the pubic area is also a major change and needs to be talked about. Also the leg hair starts thickening and there is a rapid increase in the height of both girls and boys.

Last but not the least, be patient and open to answer any question raised by your daughter. Be clear enough in your explanation and make more use of scientific terms which will make both of you comfortable while conversing.

If you do not have the correct answer for any of the questions put forth by your daughter, do not overlook or give incorrect answers. This will only confuse the child and the conversation will be of no use to her.

Talking to Your Son About Puberty

Boys may feel comfortable talking about their puberty with other males. May be the father, uncle or any other close male figure can take the responsibility of talking to the boy about the changes in his body. However, if there is no such person in his life, a trusted female can do the job. Many parents never talks to their kids about puberty. So the school in such a case must be advised to arrange a session on this subject. If you are going to talk to your boy about puberty, here are some instructions that will make your conversation better.

Like a girl, a boy also needs an assurance that whatever is happening to him is normal and there is nothing wrong in it. You should be confident enough while delivering your speech. This will make the boy believe you and won't feel awkward.

Make use of formal and scientific language which will make the explanation clearer. If you hesitate while pronouncing some words and say something different, it will only confuse the child.

Tell him that his penis and testicles will begin to grow during puberty and he will experience ejaculation. The concept of wet dreams or nocturnal emissions needs to be explained to the boy because he often gets wet dreams during puberty which makes him feel embarrassed. Nocturnal emission is nothing but the discharge of semen through the penis when the boy is asleep. The body is becoming capable of producing testosterone (male sex hormone) and there is an erection in the penis. This erection leads to ejaculation.

Tell your son about the growing hair on the face, in the armpits and the pubic area. There is also a considerable increase in the height and weight and the voice cracks and deepens.

Boys and girls both suffer from acne during puberty and it is important to tell them to take care of their body, especially the face and the skin.

Why Sex Education Determines What Type Of Person Your Child Will Grow Up To Be!

Being a mother to 2 boys, which are 13 and 10, I had always been a little bit nervous about telling my eldest boy about the facts of life. But once he got to high school and started asking questions, I knew I had probably left it too late. As he was growing up, the innocent questions tended to be skimmed around, as we always thought he was too young to know. But was he?

Sex education for children is important and needs to start with those innocent questions. Maybe not with much detail when they are 6 or 8, but certainly being truthful. As parents, it is our responsibility to help our children to develop into well adjusted men and women. Here are some other reasons to properly and timely educate your child about sex:

Sex education helps a child to wholesomely accept each part of their body and each phase of their growth. It enables them to discuss physical development without shame and embarrassment.

Sex education helps a child to understand and be satisfied with their role in life. Boys grow to be men and fathers. Girls grow to be ladies and mothers.

Sex education erases unhealthy curiosity. It takes away the mystery. Children who understand the facts and who know that their parents will truthfully discuss their questions have no cause for worry or concern. They tend to not be attracted to dirty stories and pornographic material. They immediately identify what is right and what is wrong.

Sex education does not keep children from wanting to know, but it does eliminate the need for secretive investigations and unfortunate experiences.

Wholesome information guards against serious complexes and maladjustments later on in life. It encourages a child to develop normal attitudes. Childhood misinterpretations and fears carry over into adulthood and often produce twisted, abnormal patterns in later life.

Sex education builds a child's confidence in their parents. If mothers and fathers are honest and helpful regarding matters of sex, children learn to also trust and confide in them about many other things.

Sex education given at home in dignity and authority tends to overcome and nullify the unwholesome information that reaches boys and girls from outside sources.

Sex education makes human reproduction clear and wholesome. A child should feel that having children is right. They need to know, as shown in Genesis 1:24, that God planned for each living creature to bring forth after its kind.

Sex education provides a child with sound knowledge and good attitudes which pave the way for them to happily accept new brothers and sisters. New family members are not considered 'mysterious intruders.'

Sex education, while making a child proud of their own sex, will help them appreciate the attributes and capacities of the opposite sex.

Sex education removes many sources of fear. It assures a person of their own capabilities and normalcy.

Sex education strengthens a person self-confidence. It helps him feel comfortable and well poised around others. This is true regardless of a person's age.

Sex education enables a young person reaching adulthood to make sound, mature decisions about girlfriends, boyfriends, and marriage.

Sex education lays the groundwork that helps to build a solid marriage. Young people who enter marriage with mature, wholesome attitudes and understanding are beginning on a sound premise.

Sex education prepares a child to later become a parent who can, in turn, comfortably teach their own children. Most parents who find it difficult to discuss sex matters with their children tend to be raised in homes where there was little or no proper sex education.

CHAPTER 2 EDUCATING YOUR CHILDREN ON DONOR CONCEPTION

it starts when s/he is young. A natural beginning point occurs in the context of sex education when preschoolers become aware of their bodies, gender differences, pregnancy, and birth. Or you can also start even earlier, in the form of bedtime stories when they are babies or toddlers.

An important advantage of early telling is that from the beginning it is a "normal" topic within the family. Secondly, it gives the parents a chance to begin to get comfortable with the topic; you have time to practice your conversations with your child. If you want to change how you talk about it, you get another chance.

As a child's understanding of family, reproduction and birth, and social relationships increases, so will his or her understanding of his donor conception. Children, then, needs to have their story repeated because they will focus on different aspects of it at different developmental stages.

But always, keep it simple, keep it honest. In the early years, the emphasis should be on "who our family is" of belonging and being loved. This is a story about love and connection.

'Mommy really wanted to have a baby. A very kind man helped by giving us (sperm, seeds), so Mommy could have a baby. The man who helped us is called a (sperm) donor.'

'Babies grow when a sperm and egg come together. The baby grows in mommy's tummy. Our donor gave his sperm so I could grow you.'

'One day I said 'Have I got a dad?' Then Mum told me all about how a hospital helped her to have a baby, even though she had not met the right person to be dad. I am really proud my Mum could do this and I am proud of us and our family'.

As children get older, their questions can become more specific:

What does he look like; do you have a picture? Why did he give his sperm? Will I ever meet him? Do I look like him?

During early childhood, children are working on understanding social relationships. This is the time that they will notice that there are different kinds of families. This is the time when they will probably ask, "Do I have a Daddy?" if you are a single mother or lesbian couple. It is tempting at this point to refer to the donor as the child's father or bio father. I do not recommend this. It is quite fine to use the word "donor" or "sperm donor." While the donor's connection to your child can be important to you or your child, it should not be confused with someone who is an active parent in the family.

Educating your child about how babies are made

Your child may be especially curious about the mysteries of baby making if you or someone else close to your child is expecting. Or her curiosity might be piqued by conversations with older siblings or friends at school.

Depending on what she's heard from others – some of which may be confusing or contradictory she may be trying to sort out how the baby gets inside the mother, what the baby is doing in there, and how the baby gets out.

On the other hand, some older children may show little curiosity about the subject, even if you're in your third trimester. If you are pregnant, try not to take your child's lack of interest personally: Some children this age want to know a lot and some are simply not yet interested.

How to begin talking to your grade-schooler about how babies are made

Follow your child's lead.

Answer questions as they come up and keep explanations simple. Most children don't need detailed information about the complex realities of conception, gestation, and birth.

"Wait until your child asks you," says Robert Walrath, a child psychologist at the Center for Educational and Psychological Assessment in Manchester, New Hampshire. "If children are not asking, it's not important to them."

When your child does ask, you want to have a healthy, open conversation and provide some basic information, says Susan Lipkins, a private practice child psychologist in Port Washington, New York. "As your child grows and becomes more emotionally capable, then you can go into more detail."

Ask, then tell.

Make sure you understand what your child is really asking. Linda Eyre, coauthor of How to Talk With Your Child About Sex, tells a story about a boy who asked his mother where he came from. Thinking he wanted to know about the facts of life, she sat down with him and told him everything. Then the boy told her that he was just wondering where they lived before they moved into their new house.

To avoid a misunderstanding, respond to your child's questions by asking: "What do you think?" Many children spin elaborate fantasies about how babies are created. First gets a handle on what your child is thinking. Then you can use that as a launching point for a more helpful discussion.

Use the correct language.

You can avoid confusion by using accurate terms for body parts. For example, telling a child that the baby grows inside the mother's tummy can be confusing, since that's where food goes. Instead, tell your child the baby grows in a special place inside the woman called the "womb" or "uterus."

And if you say that the father's seed grows inside the mother, the child may picture an apple seed growing into a tree inside a woman's body. Instead, you can explain that the father's sperm swim out of his body and into the mother's womb.

Tell a story.

Make your explanation into a story, with a beginning, a middle, and an end, says Lipkins. You can follow the usual plotline: The father and mother make a baby, the baby grows inside the mother's womb, and the baby comes out when he's ready.

This helps children understand that creating and growing a baby is a process that happens over time. If you're pregnant, this will also reassure your child that your pregnancy is temporary and that, when the baby grows big enough in your womb, it will come out and your child will have a sibling.

Be matter-of-fact.

Easier said than done. If you find yourself starting to get embarrassed, remember that you're just talking about a normal part of life. This book may not be "charged" for your child the way it is for adults.

On the other hand, depending on how sophisticated your child is, she may be embarrassed as well. In any case, try to be casual and straightforward in your explanations. If you show discomfort, your child may get the feeling that there's something shameful about what you're saying.

Why you should teach your kids correct names for genitals

Squeamish parents might prefer euphemisms, but the reasoning behind teaching the word "penis" instead of "dinky" is serious. Kids who know the correct terminology for genitalia are more equipped to disclose sexual abuse. Sexual health educators and child abuse experts laud the Grade 1 recommendation – and urge parents to start naming body parts properly in infancy when talking about toes, knees, elbows and ears.

"Using proper terminology is protective," says Audrey Rastin, a manager at Boost Child Abuse Prevention & Intervention in Toronto. "Kids who are comfortable talking about their bodies are more likely to be able to disclose when something worrisome or uncomfortable is happening to them."

She says that when children use incorrect terminology, they may be misunderstood. Communicating with the right words helps adults understands what is happening.

"Parents who can openly discuss and name body parts, what they do and what is appropriate can help children understand when touch or actions fall outside the range of healthy relationships, and are worrisome or abusive," Rastin says. A 1995 study found that some sexual offenders avoid children who know the correct names for their genitals: It suggests these children have also been educated about sexuality and safety.

Being able to name "private parts" using dictionary terms means victimized children can get help sooner. "The earlier the disclosure, the higher the likelihood of good healing," says Lyba Spring, a sex educator in Toronto.

Spring recounts a heartbreaking story told at a workshop by a woman who had been sexually abused as a child. Back then, the only word she knew for vulva was "cookie." "When she tried to tell a teacher about how someone wanted her cookie, the teacher told her she had to share. It's obvious that the conse uence of that was that the abuse continued. She didn't have the tools she needed to disclose."

Spring stresses that, while many parents of toddlers use "silly words" for genitals, they should be complementing them with actual terms. She suggests proper labeling when your child is learning language.

A good opportunity is bath time, when it can become routine. "As you're giving your child the building blocks, they get it – that you're willing to talk about these things," she says. "You're modelling communicating about the body."

This way, kids sense they have permission to talk freely with their parents when they do have uestions, Rastin says, adding that early, accurate naming also promotes the development of a healthy, positive body image. "We don't create pseudonyms for other body parts," she said. "No part of our body should be secret, shameful or embarrassing."

Why do so many parents hesitate to use actual terms for genitals, going with cutesy code words like "monkey" and "muffin" instead? It has to do with our cultural discomfort around talking about sex in general. In this case, it's important for parents to get over their own reticence, early.

"I have encountered parents over the years who had a strong objection to naming parts. Some of them thought that it was 'too young,'" Spring says. "They're afraid that there's somehow a direct link between naming the body parts and having sex. And they think that they can somehow maintain a child's innocence by keeping them ignorant. There's a difference between innocence and ignorance. Ignorance is dangerous."

CHAPTER 3 PROTECTING YOUR CHILD FROM CHILD ABUSE

We generally teach girls to be passive and reward them for doing so. Girls are raised to be quiet, sweet and pretty; they are never to make a 'scene.' Boys are taught, expected and praised to be tough and self-assured, even at times when something troubles them. Whenever a person is traumatized, he/she resorts to familiar behavior; for girls this behavior usually means passivity while boys usually, 'tough it out'- thinking if they are strong and unemotional, no harm can occur.

Self-protection offers a direct and effective way to empower children to help themselves. Since the perpetrator (a.k.a. sex offender) cunningly and with forethought sets the stage to perpetrate this crime in secrecy, who is better able than the child to protect him/herself? Perpetrators say they can sense a child to victimize; they sense this by the child's demeanor, body language and facial expressions. They sense the fear, the helplessness and the passivity. Perpetrators choose victims who they assume will keep the secret. Children who have experienced body boundary violations through hitting or spanking are more freﾑuently targets for sex offenders than children who haven't been hit or spanked. Children who have been spanked or hit take on the belief that their bodies are the property of others, they are more passive, fearful of authority (i.e. adults), and are less apt to protest the sexual violation or tell. No child needs to fall prey to these cunning predators.

Without knowledge of and permission to exercise self-protection, the only defense a child has against any kind of abuse is to accept the blame. A child cannot conceive the idea, "My father, uncle, mother, grandpa, grandma, aunt, brother, sister, cousin, friend, teacher, or baby-sitter is sick." Therefore, the only way to survive sexual abuse or incest is to assume that it is her/his fault. A child has unquestioning trust for everyone. "Daddy, grandpa, uncle, cousin is good; it must be me." "What is wrong with me?" More important, he/she wants and needs his/her family to be a family. She/he believes she/he stabilizes and holds the family together. She/he accepts the blame, shame, responsibility for their own abuse and an inappropriate role within the family. Her/his needs are not being met; she/he is meeting the needs of everyone else at the expense of her/his own needs.

Tragically, many survivors believe they are the only one being abused. "I thought I was the only one. I thought if I let him abuse me he would not abuse my sister." This is rarely the case. Perpetrators usually abuse more than one child and fre*uently abuse several children during a given period.

Armed with this knowledge, it is imperative to teach children to protect themselves. Teaching children: (1) good body image, (2) respecting the child's sacred body boundaries, thus avoiding leaving them vulnerable to perpetrators, (3) setting appropriate boundaries, (4) fostering their self-esteem, and (5) not keeping secrets for others, can prevent abuse or prevent the same person from repeating the abuse.

Self protection/prevention techniques can be taught in their simplest form beginning by age 2 or 2 ½. You can modify the teaching of each technique according to your child's age. However, it is critical all concepts of self-protection are taught, practiced and reinforced continuously through childhood.

l. Accept the new definition of sexual abuse or incest.

2. Accept the reality perpetrators can be persons you least expect.

3. Respect the child's sacred physical boundaries.

4. Teach and reinforce the child's right to protest uncomfortable or unacceptable touch.

5. Respect the child's perception of uncomfortable or unacceptable touch.

6. Respect the child's likes and dislikes.

7. Avoid using 'spanking or hitting' as discipline, thus your child will be less apt to be a target for sexual abuse.

8. Reinforce the child's right to protest uncomfortable or unwanted touch while doing necessary tasks such as verbally soothing the child and changing the touch.

9. Accept and practice the guidelines for 'good, appropriate' touch.

10. Intercede when others violate your child's physical boundaries or disregard likes or dislikes.

11. Teach good body image. "Your body is private, special, beautiful and perfect.'

12. Teach and practice the TELL MOMMY OR DADDY EVERYTHING--NO SECRETS RUL13. Practice appropriate suspicion-check on others' interactions with your child; trust your intuition; heed changes in your child's behavior; investigate behavioral changes and do not stop until you have a resolution.

14. If in doubt or you have the slightest suspicion your child might be a victim of sexual abuse, seek help from a professional specializing in sexual abuse recovery and Child Protective Services.

15. Ask questions, which require 'YES or NO' answers until you are confident you understand what your child is telling you.

16. Trust your child's perceptions. Children are naturally intuitive and often sense an adult's ulterior motives, although you may not suspect anything.

17. Trust and act on your intuitiveness or sixth sense.

18. If you err in evaluating the situation, make the error on the side of your child. The important factor is not that you have avoided offending potential abusers, but that you have protected your child's interest.

Saying "No" to "Touching My Private Parts" - Not Enough to Protect Your Child from Sex Offenders

The majority of parents do a good job teaching their children to beware of strangers. Yet most victims of child sexual abuse know the sex offender.

In a study of twenty adult sex offenders conducted by Jon Conte, Steven Wolf and Tim Smith; two of the key questions asked were:

1.Was there something about the child's behavior which attracted you to the child?"

Responses included:

The warm and friendly child or the vulnerable child...Friendly, showed me their panties."

"The way the child would look at me, trustingly."

"The child who was teasing me, smiling at me, asking me to do favors."

"Someone who had been a victim before--[spanking or inappropriate touch]--quiet, withdrawn, compliant. Someone, who had not been a victim would be more non-accepting of the sexual language or stepping over the boundaries of modesty... Quieter, easier to manipulate, less likely to object or put up a fight...goes along with things."

2."After you had identified a potential victim, what did you do to engage the child into sexual contact?

Responses included:

"I didn't say anything. It was at night, and she was asleep.

Talking, spending time with them, being around them at bedtime, being around them in my underwear, sitting down on the bed with them... Constantly evaluating the child's reaction... A lot of touching, hugging, kissing, snuggling." Playing, talking, giving special attention, trying to get the child to initiate contact with me... From here I would initiate different kinds of contact, such as touching the child's back, head... Testing the child to see how much she would take before she would pull away.

"Isolate them from any other people. Once alone, I would make a game of it (red light, green light with touching up their leg until they said stop). Making it fun."

"Most of the time I would start by giving them a rub down. When I got them aroused, I would take the chance and place my hand on their penis to masturbate them. If they would not object, I would take this to mean it was Okay... I would isolate them. I might spend the night with them... Physical isolation, closeness, contact are more important than verbal seduction."

We cannot ignore the sophistication of sex offenders' efforts to desensitize the child through the gradual development of a relationship with the child and progressing from non-sexual touch (touching a leg, back or head) to sexual touch. Given that 95-99 percent of sex offenders are people their victims know and trust--family members and other trusted adults--even children as young as two can be taught to know what to do to protect him/herself.

For a child who has been taught only to say, "No' to touching his/her private parts--one of the conse uences of this relationship building and desensitization process is self-blame. By the time the child realizes that his/her private parts were touched--the damage is done-- and the child may believe he/she has given consent to the abuse. He/she thinks because he/she did not say, "No" when the adult rubbed her/his back or head, he/she is to blame. It only takes one second for a sex offender to stick his tongue into a child's mouth when he is giving a 'traditional family' kiss on the lips. It only takes one second for a sex offender to put his hand up a girl's leg and touch a child's labia while she sits on his lap.

Studies reveal that teaching a child to say, "No" has little impact because it is rare a child will affect more than weak resistance against a known sex offender. Furthermore, the sex offender will usually ignore a simple, "No." The sex offender uses subtle or blatant threats, intimidating the child into compliance and silence.

Non-violation of sacred Body boundaries--to thwart the sex offender who counts on--a child who has been violated before--quiet, withdrawn, compliant. Someone, who had not been a victim, would be more non-accepting of the sexual language or stepping over the boundaries of modesty... Quieter, easier to manipulate, less likely to object or put up a fight...goes along with things."

Good, Appropriate Touch

Appropriate Body Boundaries

Good Body Image

Tell Mommy and Daddy Everything--No Secrets Rule

Appropriate Suspicion

Appropriate Suspicion (intuition, a.k.a. sixth sense) alone when acted upon empowers the child to thwart the majority of would-be sex offenders. Coupled with the other five techniques--your child is well prepared to stop every sex offender in their tracks.

Trusting and acting on your intuition or sixth sense and allowing your child to trust his/her intuition is paramount to protecting children from sex offenders, no matter whether they are family members, family friends, doctors, dentists, teachers, etc. Children are naturally intuitive and often sense an adult's ulterior motives, although you may not suspect anything.

We need to accept the reality that no one can be considered exempt from being a sex offender, including all family members. As a parent, be appropriately suspicious and trust your intuition. If you err in evaluating a situation, make the error on the side of your child. The important factor is not that you have avoided offending someone, but that you have protected your child until you can investigate further.

Another important aspect of child protection is taking responsibility.

"Those who ignore the past are condemned to repeat it." -Jean-Paul Sartre

"We are not only responsible for what we do, but also, for what we don't do." -Voltaire

"Every choice we make, every thought and feeling we have, is an act of power that has biological, environmental, social, personal and global consequences." -Caroline Myss

Types of child abuse every parent should know

Child abuse pertains to either doing or failing to do things to/for a child (under the age of 16, which is the age of consent), which may result in immediate harm to him/her, or may leave a deep impact on the child's mind. The term 'abuse' refers to maltreatment, deliberately or unknowingly, that may yield crucial conseZuences, and sometimes even be fatal. Child abuse is, in any form, a serious offense, and many countries have defined legislations that facilitate the fight against this grievous crime. Any kind of physical, mental or sexual mistreatment of a child amounts to child abuse. Leaving a child in a state of neglect or abandoning him altogether are also forms of the same.

The Federal Child Abuse Prevention and Treatment Act (CAPTA) defines child abuse as:

Any recent act or failure to act on the part of a parent or caretaker, which results in death, serious physical and emotional harm, sexual abuse or exploitation.

An act or failure to act, which presents an imminent risk of serious harm.

Every state in the U.S. has its own definition of child abuse, based on the basic framework provided by the CAPTA. These definitions, along with the laws against child abuse, have been incorporated in civil as well as criminal statutes of the respective states.

Child abuse can take place anywhere - at home, school, public places - wherever a child goes or interacts with others. It can take several forms, and cause long-lasting scars on the body of the child, as well as the mind. The various types are as under:

Physical Abuse: Causing any kind of physical injury to the child is known as physical abuse. This may be done by parents, teachers or a third person, and often takes place in the name of teaching the child to behave properly. Parents and teachers who are involved in this kind of child abuse generally do not tend to realize that this is actually a criminal/civil offense and an unethical act, which might harm the mentality of the child in the long run. On the other hand, a child is physically harmed intentionally in order to cause him an injury. In this sense, the case of Mary Ellen Wilson, which was the first ever reported case of child abuse in America, is a classic example. It took place in New York, in 1874. Mary was physically tortured, tied, and beaten up by her step-mother everyday, and there were deep scars on her body when she was rescued. Such cases happen even today, and protecting children from such pedo paths become a big challenge, as not all such cases are reported. Some signs that point towards physical abuse in children include the presence of cuts, bruises, and other injuries on the body, fearfulness, being over-alert and shocked at minor things, deliberate attempts to cover the injury marks, etc.

Mental Abuse: This is also called psychological or emotional abuse. Causing harm to the child's psyche that may affect him in the long run amounts to mental abuse. This type of abuse tends to adversely affect, and sometimes even completely negates the all-round development of the child, especially in the social sphere. The immediate consequence of mental abuse is the loss of confidence or rise of a pessimistic attitude in the child. Cases of mental abuse display signs of two totally extreme psychological conditions - the child may either become too aggressive or he may become extremely passive. Various forms of mental abuse, including humiliating the child in front of others; comparing him to his friends or others; shouting or threatening the child, or not talking to him at all, and exposing him to the abuse of some other person or animal, might adversely affect him. Mental child abuse can happen at home as well as in school. Sometimes, parents who are over-protective about their child also tend to emotionally abuse in the course of disciplining him/her. Children also get abused because of the stress or tension that their parents might be undergoing. Mental abuse of children is rarely a deliberate attempt on the part of the abuser; it happens due to the presence of certain circumstances, under which a person tends to unknowingly harm a child. This, however, does not mean that it can never be intentional.

Sexual Abuse: This is when an older person uses the body of a child for his sexual satisfaction. Cases of child sexual abuse are being reported everyday all over the world, with the instances increasing at an alarming rate. Things amounting to sexual abuse of a child include provoking or forcing a child into a sexual act, indecent revealing of his genitals for one's sexual stimulation, and either showing him pornography, or using him for the same. Child rape is the most horrific form of child sexual abuse, which can prove to be fatal, in most cases. Sexual abuse affects the child, both physically and psychologically. Several forms of physical harm which may be incurred, include damage to internal organs, bleeding, exposure to sexually transmitted diseases (STDs), several neurological conditions such as improper functioning of the brain, untimely pregnancy in case of girls, and death in many cases. Psychologically, the child may face conditions such as mental trauma, depression, loss of self-confidence or low self-esteem, anxiety or symptoms of self-destruction, that may eventually lead to suicide. It is a pity that a large number of such cases go unreported every year, as many children who undergo this trauma are either scared to tell the elders or are not taken seriously. As discussed in this book, It is the duty of the parents to talk freely about this evil to their children, and make them aware of it, so that they can understand what they are going through if they are ever subjected to it in the future, thus enabling them to oppose it.

Child Neglect: Child neglect refers to depriving a child of his basic necessities of food, clothing, shelter, hygiene, and proper care. It amounts to child abuse when it reaches a level where the chances of harm to the child may surface. There are varied reasons for child neglect. It may take place if a parent or a guardian is either physically or psychologically unfit to take care of the child and provide him with his basic needs. It can also happen in cases where the parents or guardians are addicted to alcohol or drugs, due to which they are unable to care for their children. Apathy or lack of concern is another reason for child neglect, especially in case of step-children. Poverty can also cause child neglect, as it results in the failure to fulfill the child's basic needs. A neglected child may suffer from physical as well as emotional problems. One of the most visible and apparent physical signs of neglect is the skinny or bloated appearance of a child, which is a result of undernourishment. He may also suffer from physical disorders such as asthma, hypertension, or various kinds of allergies. On the psychological front, he may suffer from issues such as depression, stress, violent behavior, and aggression, among other behavioral disorders. However, the effects will depend on the degree of neglect that the child has had to face during his childhood, and his own willpower.

Substance Abuse: Substance abuse refers to exposing a child to any substance or its manufacture, that is not suitable for him or may have an adverse effect on his health, immediately as well as in the long run. This generally pertains to harmful substances such as tobacco, alcohol, and drugs. Exposure to these substances may lead to addiction in children, which in turn may harm their health in many ways. Children facing substance abuse at a young age may go on to become hardcore alcoholics or drug addicts, or even indulge in anti-social activities in the future, which in any case is not good for the society. So, substance abuse has been classified as one of the forms of child abuse in the U.S., and has serious legal conse?uences.

Child Exploitation: Child exploitation is prevalent in some form or the other throughout the world, especially in third world and other developing countries. Child exploitation involves evils such as recruiting children to perform laborious tasks, indulging them in prostitution, acts of child trafficking, and so on. All these acts amount to social and moral evil, and are punishable offenses. People subjected to exploitation as children may turn out to be anti-social elements or child exploiters themselves. One needs to understand that children need to play and study during their childhood, and should not be made to succumb to the difficulties of life at such an early age, as such things tend to make a deep impact on their lives.

Nowadays, the Internet has gained ground everywhere and is easily accessible to everybody, be it a child or an adult. In such a scenario, it is very difficult to keep a check on instances of child abuse that tend to take place every now and then through the world wide web, which could include child pornography, Internet bullying, conversation that is laced with sexual content in chat rooms, and so on. There are a number of cyber laws that have been framed in order to control such kinds of cyber crimes, but the Internet is a huge world. It is thus advisable to monitor such happenings at homes, schools, and Internet cafes so that they can be reduced.

It is very important for a child to understand that he/she is being abused. This, then becomes the duty of the elders, especially the parents, who need to educate the child in this regard. Talking freely about child abuse in general, and sexual abuse in particular, with children, is a good way of communicating to them the evils that are involved. Children needs to be sure that no matter what problem they get into, their parents are always there for them. Parents need to trust their children completely, which in turn will help them gain the trust of the children. It is only in an atmosphere of absolute trust and security that children will be able to approach their parents or elders and talk to them freely, in case, they have been abused. When the parents assure the child that it was the right thing that the child did by approaching and reporting to them, it will instill confidence within the child that he has support and help, whenever needed. But in cases where abuse is of a severe nature, it is always advisable to take the child to a counselor, who will help get rid of the feeling of guilt and fright, and aid in coping with the negative emotions.

Child abuse, in any form, is injurious to the future of a child. Physical scars heal with the passage of time, but mental scars don't. They leave a permanent impact on the mind of an abused child, who is likely to grow up into an individual with many psychological problems (abandonment issues, anti-social tendencies). Sometimes, the abused becomes the abuser, and often he becomes so aggressive that he poses a threat to society. In some cases, he becomes a dominating kind of person, wanting to get all things done in his own way, and in other cases, he becomes a staunch pessimist, who tends to take everything in a negative light. He might also lack the ability to take the simplest of decisions on his own. In certain cases, he may even become a hardcore criminal, always wanting to be at war with society. Whichever the case may be, child abuse kills the child in a kid. Some learn to cope with its effects and bring about a semblance of normalcy in their lives, while others continue to suffer from the severe effects of the act(s), and can never be the same again. It is to prevent this, that treatment in the form of counseling and support becomes an absolute necessity.

Signs that You May Notice if your child is abuse

Each type of child abuse will leave behind some signs and if noticed carefully, they can be identified.

Physical Signs

The child suffers from unexplained bruises, burns, or black eyes

Freꝗuently suffers from bone fractures

The child remains absent from school for long periods

Fading bruises or marks of trauma on the child's body

The child avoids the parents or caregivers

Does not like going home after school

Is frightened when approached by adults

Parents give conflicting explanations for the injuries

Parents or caregivers themselves have a history of child abuse

Begins to have problems in school with grades and other children

Anti-social behavior

Emotional Signs

The child begins to develop an extremely complaining or demanding behavior

The child becomes passive or aggressive all of a sudden

The child shows infantile behavior like head banging, sucking thumb, eating hair, rocking, etc.

Attempts suicide

Begins to use self-depreciating words like 'I'm worthless', 'I'm stupid', etc.

Begins to say 'I deserve this' when hurt

Suddenly starts stammering or shuttering

Shows physical, mental, and emotional downfall

Signs of Neglect

The child is always hungry

Shows poor personal hygiene

The clothes are too old or dirty or ragged

The child is forever feeling tired

Suffers from untreated medical problems

Compulsive scavenging

Has no social contact

Turns destructive

Sexual Signs

The child begins to have difficulty walking and sitting

Starts bed wetting or having nightmares

The child suffers from change in appetite, either begins to eat alot or stops eating altogether

Begins to show interest or has knowledge about sexual acts

Avoids taking part in a physical activity or becomes overly paranoid about changing clothes around others

Develops an STD or becomes pregnant, especially in the case of girls under 14 years

Runs away from home

Is scared or uncomfortable when a particular person is around.

CHAPTER 4- DON'T KEEP YOUR CHILD WONDERING HOW MUMMY AND DADDY DO IT

Sex is a fascinating thing even in childhood; and sexual feelings are an integral part and experience of growing up. It is, therefore, a natural and healthy evolution that should not be shrouded in secrecy, as many parents, do.

Secrecy and made-up stories designed to shield children from the truth about their sexuality can only cause more problems, confusion and guilt feelings. Instead, children should be gently and lovingly taught and made familiar with the truth about sex, so that they can grow up into positive, healthy, mature and balanced personalities. Lack of child sex education creates more peeping-toms, porn addicts, rapists and other pervert sex personalities.

With the unfortunate calamity of explicit sex and internet porn upon us, it is even more the duty of parents to properly prepare their children for life in the larger society. Being naturally curious and mentally alert, children are fast and easy learners. Child sex education can therefore begin at a very tender age, long before a child grows up and begins to get exposed to the negative influences of the internet.

Couples should make sex education for their child an integral attribute of a truthful and disciplined family relationship. When couples display intimacy and lack of inhibition about sex and nakedness, they send a direct and sensitive message to the child. You have nothing to lose because already in many families, it is not uncommon for children to overhear or even 'catch' their parents making love.

Therefore, while the higher mysteries and deeper intimacies of sexual union should be reserved for later years, a child should be gradually introduced to the ordinary mechanics of love-making and allowed to enter into the parent's circle of love; instead of being shut out completely and left to wonder how daddy and mommy do it.

Here are tips to get you started with educating your child about his/her sexuality:

Couples can deliberately leave the bedroom door open or ajar while expressing intimacy.

Call upon your child to bring or take something away while you are expressing intimacy.

Take your child into bed with you and allow him or her watch as you share intimacy.

A mother should feel relaxed breast-feeding her baby while her husband makes love to her.

A couple should have no inhibition having their child watch as they share intimate embrace.

If intelligently applied, these situations will create an atmosphere of love and openness that helps you to gently and lovingly pull your child into the sacred circle of sex. That way, you naturally and positively initiate your child into his or her sexuality. Your child will love you for it, and be ever grateful for such loving, reassuring, and indelible experience.

CHAPTER 5- YOUR CHILD SEXUAL DEVELOPMENT

Child sexual development is part of a child's healthy growth and development. A parent's response towards their child's sexual situations and questions heavily influence a child's attitude toward sexuality and can influence whether a child feels comfortable discussing sexual issues with their parents into their teen years.

As a child grows and develops they are learning how to interact with others in a socially acceptable way. One of the first steps in sexual development is the process a child goes through in developing gender identity; which is the realization that they are either a boy or a girl. They are also developing an understanding of different types of relationships between people, seeing the difference between the relationship they have with mommy and daddy, as apposed to friends, grandparents etc. These are the basic foundations of how a child's sexuality develops.

Parents and caregivers influence sexual development indirectly as they interact with children. The manner in which they speak to children, how they cuddle and play with them, affect a child's sexual development. As children grow, the observations they make about the relationships around them, and the relationships they develop with family members and friends also affect their sexual development.

In early childhood, sexual development includes when a child becomes curious about where babies come from. They may also explore other children's and other adult's bodies out of curiosity. For some children, genital touching increases, especially when the child is tired or upset. At this age of sexual development, masturbation is associated with relaxation and desire but is considered non-sexual if the child doesn't associate it with sex.

Child sexual development in a child around age four also includes a sense of modesty about their bodies. They are beginning to develop an understanding about the difference between private behavior (such as changing, going to the bathroom or showering) and public behavior.

In order to maintain healthy growth and development in terms of sexual development of a child, a parent needs to open the doors of communication early. As children show curiosity, parents should explain in simple terms the differences between men and women and explain how babies are made.

Healthy child sexual development includes using the correct terms for sexual body parts. Parents need to learn to talk to their children about these body parts without making their children feel like they are doing something bad.

It is also important at this stage of sexual development to explain to a child that touching their sexual organs is normal, but that that is something to be done in privacy. It is also very important to talk with children about their right to privacy, and how to say 'no' to unwanted touching.

As a child reaches the school age phase of their child sexual development, it is important to discuss sexuality in more depth. Parents should explain that people experience sexual pleasure in a number of ways, and that it is normal to have sexual thoughts and fantasies. Children should also be aware of the dangers of sexual predators.

Although the topic of sexual education is controversial, the fact is that there is no stopping the progress of child sexual development, which inevitably leads to puberty and adolescence. Keeping the lines of communication open allows your child the freedom to develop a healthy sexual identity.

CONCLUSION

For many parents,the very thought of discussing sex with their children causes sweaty palms and sends chills down their spine.

"How will I know what to say?"

"When is the right age?"

"What if they laugh at me?"

"Should I use some sort of book?"

These are just a few questions parents have asked me while serving as a church youth director and counselor. While it can seem awkward at first, if you are intentional about the sex talk, you can create a positive rapport with your child. Discussing sex with your kids is more than just education. It creates an openness within your communication. You want to send the message that "If I can talk to my parents about sex, then I can talk to them about anything."

What not to do:

1. Don't embarrass them

This can happen when parents discuss their own sexual experiences with their children. The teens I see will share more about sex with me than their parents because they have felt embarrassed by their parents' behaviors. Your role is to be a facilitator of sexual discussion, not a reporter.

2. Don't lecture them and attempt to make them conform to your standards

No one likes to be controlled by another person. This is especially true with teens. If they feel controlled, most will likely say one thing to your face and do the opposite. There is no way that you are going to "make" your teens behave the way you want them to, as no other adult can make you do something you do not want to do. Rather, use this time to have serious discussions with your teen about healthy sexuality. Have a true dialogue with them, raising their awareness of the consequences of their decisions.

3. Don't wait until your children are adolescents to begin talking about sex

What is the right age to start talking about sex? When your children start to ask questions. Even preschoolers will ask where babies come from. Answer them in a simple matter of fact manner. To tell them they will have to wait until they are older stifles their desire to ask any further questions. Sex education needs to start as early as elementary school and continue through pre-adolescence, teen and young adulthood years.

What to do

Be an example

Teens are great at "doing as you do, not as you say." Many teens that I have counseled are frustrated by the "double standards" set by their parents.

Be Straight Forward

Use proper terms for the penis, vagina, orgasm, and other parts of the body. To use slang can send the message that you are not taking this seriously, so why should they?

Discuss healthy boundaries with them.

Ask them what they think their physical boundaries should be. Ask if they think there will be any future conseuences to their behavior. Help them to think through their choices. Sex is more than just a physical pleasure but will also have emotional consequences as well.

Be discreet when your kids have friends over or spending the night.

I think this one is self-explanatory!

Be age appropriate.

Begin with a little bit of information, and then continue as they are able to handle it. There is no need to give the full description to kids if they cannot understand it.

Stay in touch

Educate yourself on what the sexual issues are that your children may be facing. Sometimes they may come right out and tell you. Other times you will need to be aware of what is going on in contemporary youth culture, and issues at their school.

Having the Sex Talk with your child can be something that enhances your relationship, rather than being scary.

15269469R00032

Printed in Great Britain
by Amazon